OPTIONS TRADING FOR
BEGINNERS

A Beginners Guide To The Most Useful Tools, Strategies, And
Tricks To Earn Money With Options Trading

MARK KRATTER

2

content within this book has been derived from various sources. Please consult a licensed professional before attempting any techniques outlined in this book.

By reading this document, the reader agrees that under no circumstances is the author responsible for any losses, direct or indirect, which are incurred as a result of the use of information contained within this document, including, but not limited to, errors, omissions, or inaccuracies.

Table of Contents

Introduction

If you have spent any time looking at the world of investing, you may have heard about options at one point or another. They are sometimes going to seem pretty overwhelming to think about, but if you know a few key points that come with them, options can be pretty easy to understand. Options can be seen as another class of assets, just like mutual funds, ETFs, bonds, and stocks. And when the investor properly uses them, they can offer you some unique advantages that trading with the other assets just can't. You can purchase options like most other asset classes, simply by using an investment account from a brokerage. You may want to do a bit of research with these ahead of time to ensure you find the right brokerage firm for your needs. Options can be a powerful tool because they are going to do some wonders when it comes to enhancing your portfolio.

Options can provide you with this advantage as the offer a source of additional income, greater protection and further leverage. Based on the situation, you will find some sort of options contract that can provide you with an adequate alternative. In turbulent times, options are a great means of protecting your portfolio against sharp and unexpected declines.

In addition to protecting some of your personal assets, options are sometimes used to generate a recurring income. And some investors will choose to use these in a more speculative purpose, such as wagering on the direction that a stock will take. Just like with any of the other choices that you make with investing, options will involve some risks and you must fully understand these and know how to avoid them as much as possible. This is why any time you want to start trading options with a broker, there is going to be some kind of disclaimer like the following to help you know about the risk with options: Options involve risks and are not suitable for everyone. Options trading can be speculative in nature and carry substantial risk of loss. Only invest in risk capital. Options are going to belong to a larger group of securities that are known as derivatives. This is a word that many investors are going to associate with excessive risk-taking. In the past, Warren Buffett has even referred to these derivatives as a weapon of mass destruction when it comes to the stock market.

When you learned to drive, you didn't just jump in the car and turn it on. Instead, someone walked you through exactly what to do before you started the car. You were told what the stick-shift or automatic PRNDL (Park-Reverse-Neutral-Drive-Low) was for. You were told how to move the mirrors, what was forward and reverse, and other buttons in the car. Before you invest in the stock market, you need to walk, not run. You need a guide that tells you how things work, so you avoid making costly mistakes. As long as you know how something works, you don't have to be afraid of the reality of it. Many people do not understand investing, so the stock market scares them. The reality is—you just need to know how it works, the parts that make it work, and you can set up an investment strategy that works.

A stock is usually referred to as a share. It is a share in a company that is looking for investors. These investors provide capital for the company to grow the company. When a company first offers shares, it is called an IPO or Initial Public Offering. The share price is set on the estimated worth of the company, as well as the number of shares available for sale.

For the shares to be publicly offered, a company needs to be listed on a stock exchange, like the NYSE (New York Stock Exchange). Traders and investors can then buy and sell stocks, but the company will only make money with the IPO. After the IPO is over, it is simply businessmen, individuals, and investors trading the stocks between themselves to make a profit and dividends.

Chapter 1. Options Trading Basics

What Are Stock Options

To get an understanding of the meaning of stock options, we first have to know the meaning of the two words independently.

Stock refers to:

- The total money a company has from selling shares to individuals.

- A portion of the ownership of the company that can be sold to members of the public

Option (finance) refers to:

A contract that provides the buyer with the right, though not the obligation, to sell or buy an asset at an agreed-upon strike price at a specified date based on the type of option

Now that we know the meaning of both stocks and options, we can easily define stock options. We can define the term in the following ways:

Stock options provide an investor with the right to sell or buy a stock at a set price and date.

The stock option can also refer to an advantage in the form of an opportunity provided by a company to any employee to buy shares in a company at an agreed-upon fixed price or a discount.

Stock options have been a topic of interest in recent years. We are having more and more people engaging in options trading. The profitability of stock options has resulted in a lot of debates. Some say it's a scam; others claim that it is not a worthy investment while others say that they are minting millions from it. All these speculations draw us to one question, which is what are stock options? For us to accurately answer this question, we will have to go through stock options keenly. We will be required to know all about it and what it entails. This information makes it easy to make judgments with actual facts as opposed to using assumptions. You will get to say something that you can actually back up. Having knowledge gives you an added advantage and places you in a powerful position.

Understanding Stock Options

For us to understand stock options, we consider the following:

Strike Price

For one to know if a stock can be exercised, they will need to consider the strike price. By the time an option gets to the expiration date, there is a price that it is expected to have. This price should be lower or higher than the stock price, and it is what we refer to as the strike price of an underlying asset. If as an investor, you predict that the value of the stock will increase, you can purchase a call option at the set strike price. When it comes to putting options, the strike price will be the price at which an asset is traded by the option buyer by the time the contract expires. The strike price can also be referred to as the exercise price. It is a major factor to consider while establishing the option value. Depending on when the options are carried out, the strike price will differ. As an investor, it is good to keep track of the strike price since it helps in identifying the quality of an investment.

Styles

There are two main option styles. These are European and American options styles. If you intend to engage in options trading, it is advisable to equip yourself with knowledge of the various styles. As you analyze the styles, you will identify those that work for you and those that do not. You will also find that some styles are easier to learn and handle as opposed to others. You can decide to engage in the one that is convenient for you and avoid engaging in the style that you have difficulties understanding.

The American style option allows one to exercise a trade any period between the time of purchase and the time a contract expires. Most traders engage in this style due to its convenience. It allows one to carry out a trade any period within which a contract is considered to be valid. The European style option is not commonly used as

14

compared to the American style. In the European option style, a trader can only exercise their options during the expiration date. If you are not an expert in options trading, I would advise you to avoid using the European style.

Expiration date

An expiration date refers to the period in which a contract is regarded as worthless. Stocks have expiration dates. The period between when they were purchased and the expiry date, indicate the validity of an option. As a trader, you are expected to utilize the contracts to your advantage, within this time frame. You can trade as much as you can and get high returns within the period of buying and the period of expiry. Learn to utilize the time provided adequately. If you are not careful, the option may expire before you get a chance to exercise it.

We have may beginners who assume this factor and end up making heavy losses. You will be required to be keen while engaging in the stock market. Forgetting to look into the expiry date may result in your stocks being regarded as worthless without getting a chance of investing in them. In some rare cases, the stocks are exercised during the expiry date. This is common in the European option. I would not encourage a beginner to engage in this type of option. It is tricky and could lead to a loss if you are not careful while carrying out the trade.

Contacts

Contracts refer to the amount of shares an investor is intending to purchase. One hundred shares of an underlying asset are equal to one contract. Contracts aid in establishing the value of s stock. Contracts tend to be valuable before the expiry date. After the expiry date, a contract can be regarded as worthless. Knowing this will help you discover the best time to exercise a contract. In a case where a trader purchases ten contracts, he or she gets to 10 $ 350 calls. When the stock prices go above $ 350, at the expiry trade, the trader gets the chance to buy or sell 1000 shares of their stock at $350. This happens regardless of the stock price at that particular time. In an event whereby the stock is lower than $350, the option will expire worthlessly. This will result in making a complete loss as an investor. You will lose the whole amount you used to purchase options, and there is no way of getting it back. If you intend to invest in options trading, it is good to become aware of the contracts and how you can exercise them for a profitable options trading outcome.

Premium

The premium refers to the money used to purchase options. You can obtain the premium by multiplying the call price and the number of contracts by 100. The '100' is the number of shares per contract. This is more like the investment made by the trader expecting great returns. While investing, you will expect that the investment you chose to engage in will result in a profitable outcome. No one gets in business anticipating a loss. You find that one is always hopeful that the investment they have chosen to engage in will be beneficial. You will constantly look forward to getting the best out of a trade.

The above factors tell us more about stocks. In case you were stuck and didn't fully understand what stocks entail, now you have a better understanding. You will come across numerous terms when you decide to engage in stocks. Do not let the terms scare you; they are mostly things you knew, but just didn't know that they go by those terms. We have many people who are quite investing in stocks, just because they could not understand the various terms being used. This should not be the case. You can take some time to go through the terms and understand what they entail carefully.

Options in Stock Market

Stock options are not as hard as people make them appear. At times people try to make them seem difficult, yet it is an easy thing that can be grasped by almost everyone. As a beginner, do not be discouraged into thinking that options trading is a difficult investment. You will be surprised how easy it is, and you will wonder why you never invested in it sooner. When engaging in stock options, there are four factors the investors will have to consider. Putting these factors into consideration will have a positive impact on their trade.

The Right, But Not the Obligation

What comes in your mind when you read this statement? Well, when we talk or rights, we mean that you have the freedom to purchase a certain type of option. When we talk of obligation, we are referring to the fact that one does not have a legal authority to exercise a duty. Options do not give traders a legal authority to carry out a duty. This means that there is freedom to trade, but it is not legally mandated.

Buying or Selling

As a trader, you are given the right to purchase or trade an option. There are two types of stock that one can choose from. We have the put option and the call option. Both differ and have their individual pros and cons. If you intend trading in options, it is important that you equip yourself with adequate knowledge before trading or purchasing stocks. This information will have an impact on your expected income. The stocks you choose to buy or sell will dictate if you will earn high returns or if you will end up making a loss.

Set Price

There is a certain price that has been set to exercise the option. The price will vary depending on the option type. Some stock options tend to be valued more than other options. There are a number of factors that will influence the price of options.

Expiry Date

The expiry date is when a contract will be considered useless. Stock options have an expiry date. The date is set to determine the value of an option. Any period before the expiration date, a contact is regarded as being valid. This means that it can be utilized to generate income at any point before the expiry date. When it gets to the expiry date, a trader has no power to exercise the option. This is as a result of the contract being regarded as worthless. As an investor, it is good to constantly ensure that your investment is within the duration of its validity.

Chapter 2.　Strategies for Beginners

I have to admit it -- I'm a covered calls junkie.

I've been selling covered calls since 1996 and have made hundreds of thousands of dollars in the process.

After all these years, I'm still amazed that someone is willing to pay me for the chance to take my stock off my hands for a profit.

There is a common misconception that trading options is inherently riskier than trading stocks. It's easy to see where this misconception comes from: many people do indeed trade options in a reckless manner. Options can be used to magnify returns on the upside, and the downside. In inexperienced or greedy hands, this can be a recipe for disaster.

Most of these reckless traders are buying options. The strategy that you are about to learn involves selling options.

Here's how it works:

You buy a stock, and then enter into a contract ("you sell some call options"). This contract says that you will get paid some cash today (the "premium"), in exchange for giving up the stock's potential upside past a certain point. Maybe you buy 100 shares of stock XYZ at 20.00 and agree to give up all potential upside past 21.00 ("the strike price"). In exchange, you get paid $1.00 per share (or $100, since you own 100 shares).

Let's review what just happened: you bought a stock at 20.00 and immediately got paid 1.00. In effect, you have only paid 19.00 for the stock.

If the stock goes to zero the next day, you lose 19.00 (or $1,900 since you own 100 shares). On the other hand, if you had bought the stock without entering into the contract, and the stock went to zero the next day, you would have lost 20.00 (or $2,000 since you own 100 shares).

Hopefully this shows how covered calls can actually decrease the risk of a long stock position.

So, what are the risks associated with covered calls?

Risk #1: Lost upside

Risk #2: See risk #1

The riskiest thing about covered calls is that you miss out on a stock's appreciation past a certain point.

If you sold covered calls on Apple (AAPL) back when it was $100 (pre-split) and then it ran up past $800, you left a pretty big chunk of change on the table.

But what if instead you held General Electric (GE) in your account over the past 2 years? (I'm writing this in May 2015.) You have watched the stock bounce between 23 and 28, pretty much going nowhere. You've been paid a small dividend while you waited but have otherwise been treading water. In this case, selling covered calls on the position would have generated significantly higher returns.

The moral?

Don't apply the covered calls strategy to stocks that you think will appreciate sharply in the near future.

Covered calls work best on stocks that are trading sideways, or slightly up.

If you own a stock in your long-term portfolio, and you don't think it is going anywhere over the short term, covered calls are an excellent strategy to generate some monthly income while you wait.

A Step-by-Step Guide to Selling Covered Calls

back to top

First, let's go over some basic terminology.

A "call option" (or just a "call") is a contract that gives you the right to buy a stock at a certain price, over a certain period of time, until the option expires. If you own a call option ("are long a call"), you have the right to buy the stock, but you don't have to buy the stock.

So, for example, let's look at a KO June 41.00 call.

"KO" is simply the ticker of the underlying stock, in this case, Coke ("The Coca-Cola Company").

"June" is what is called the option's "expiration date." This is the month when the options contract expires. Expiration usually occurs at the end of the day on the 3rd Friday of the month, or 19 June 2015 in this case.

"41.00" is the "strike price": this is the price at which the owner of the call option has the right to purchase the stock (or "call it away" from its owner, hence the name "call").

If you buy a call ("if you are long a call"), you are betting that the stock will move up in price.

If you sell a call ("if you are short a call"), you are betting that the stock will stay roughly where it is or move down in price.

If you sell a call, and the underlying stock moves up a lot in price, you can lose a lot of money, and end up having to buy back the call at a higher price. If you are just short a call, it is called a "naked call." It is a naked call because you are "exposed" to sharp up moves in the stock.

Covered calls are much safer.

When trading covered calls, we buy a stock and then sell an equivalent amount of call options at a strike price that is just above where we bought the stock. If the stock moves up sharply, you will lose money on the short call position, but you will make back an equal amount on the long stock position. In other words, you are "covered" and don't have the huge risk of loss that you do with naked calls.

There are times when it can be advantageous to sell naked calls, but that is an advanced strategy, and the subject for another book.

For now, you should stick to covered calls.

Let's look at a real example to make this clear.

As I'm writing this, Coke (KO) is trading at $40.94 per share.

I like Coke at this price, and so I decide to sell covered calls on it.

To make the numbers easy, let's assume that I have enough money to buy 1,000 shares of Coke.

If you are trading a small account ($5,000 or less), there is a special way of doing covered calls that you can learn about here:

So, if I have the capital, I buy 1,000 shares at 40.94. This costs me $40,940, plus a $4.95 commission (if you're using TradeKing), for a grand total of $40,944.95.

Now I immediately decide to sell calls against this stock position.

To get an options quote, I navigate to Yahoo Finance, enter the symbol KO, then click on "Options" in the left-hand menu.

This link should take you there:

http://finance.yahoo.com/q/op?s=KO+Options

Next, I go to the drop-down menu for the date, and select June 12, 2015, which is about 30 days from today.

I choose the strike price that is just above my purchase price: this strike price is 41.00.

I've already chosen an expiration date from the drop-down: June 12, 2015. This is the date that the contract ends ("expires").

Here's what it looks like on Yahoo Finance today. If you'd like to expand the image, just double-click on it:

I've circled the strike price ("41") as well as the bid price ("0.57"). The bid is the price that the market is willing to pay for a call option. Since I am selling calls, I should set my limit order to the bid price, if I would like my order to be filled right away.

26

Each call option covers 100 shares of stock. So, if I now own 1,000 shares of Coke, I need to sell 10 (1,000 divided by 100) call options.

So, I sell 10 call options to the bid (use the order type "sell to open"), and my order is filled. If I used TradeKing.com, I was charged a commission of $4.95 base rate plus 10 contracts times $0.65 per contract, or $11.45. I sold 10 calls, and so my account was credited with 10 calls times 100 shares per call times 0.57 (the price at which I sold the calls), or $570.

My net credit after the commission is $570.00 minus $11.45, or $558.55.

I get to keep this $558.55 ("the premium") no matter what happens.

I am still long the 1,000 shares of Coke that I bought.

And I am "short" 10 call options in my account. I am "short" because I sold something that I didn't have. Don't worry about this for now.

As the price of the stock trades up, the shares of Coke will gain in value, while the short call position loses roughly an equal amount (more on this later).

As the price of the stock trades down, the shares of Coke will lose value, while the short call position will make money.

As we mentioned before, covered calls work best in a flat to slightly up market.

Chapter 3.   Pricing   and   Volatility Strategies

While the stock market has long term trends that investors rely on fairly well as the years and decades go by, over the short term the stock market is highly volatile. By that, we mean that prices are fluctuating up and down and doing so over short time periods. Volatility is something that long-term investors ignore. It's why you will hear people that promote conservative investment strategies suggesting that buyers use dollar cost averaging. What this does is it averages out the volatility in the market. That way you don't risk making the mistake of buying stocks when the price is a bit higher than it should be, because you'll average that out by buying shares when it's a bit lower than it should be.

In a sense, over the short term, the stock market can be considered as a chaotic system. So from one day to the next, unless there is something specific on offer, like Apple introducing a new gadget that investors are going to think will be a major hit, you can't be sure what the stock price is going to be tomorrow or the day after that. An increase on one day doesn't mean more increases are coming; it might be followed by a major dip the following day.

For example, at the time of writing, checking Apple's stock price, on the previous Friday it bottomed out at $196. Over the following days, it went up and down several times, and on the most recent close, it was $203. The movements over a short-term period appear random, and to a certain extent, they are. It's only over the long term that we see the actual direction that Apple is heading.

Of course, Apple is at the end of a ten-year run that began with the introduction of the iPhone and iPad. It's a reasonable bet that while it's a solid long-term investment, the stock probably isn't going to be moving enough for the purposes of making good profits over the short term from trades on call options (not to mention the per share price is relatively high).

The truth is volatility is actually a friend of the trader who buys call options. But it's a friend you have to be wary of because you can benefit from volatility while also getting in big trouble from it.

The reason stocks with more volatility are the friend of the options trader is that in part the options trader is playing a probability game. In other words, you're looking for stocks that have a chance of beating the strike price you need in order to make profits. A volatile stock that has large movements has a greater probability of not only passing your strike price but doing so in such a fashion that it far exceeds your strike price enabling you to make a large profit.

Of course, the alternative problem exists – that the stock price will suddenly drop. That is why care needs to be a part of your trader's toolkit. A stock with a high level of volatility is just as likely to suddenly drop in price as it is to skip right past your strike price.

31

Moreover, while you're a beginner and might get caught with your pants down, volatile stocks are going to attract experienced options traders. That means that the stock will be in high demand when it comes to options contracts. What happens when there is a high demand for something? The price shoots up. In the case of call options, that means the stock will come with a higher premium. You will need to take the higher premium into account when being able to exercise your options at the right time and make sure the price is high enough above your strike price that you don't end up losing money.

Traders take some time to examine the volatility of a given stock over the recent past, but they also look into what's known as implied volatility. This is a kind of weather forecast for stocks. It's an estimate of the future price movements of a stock, and it has a large influence on the pricing of options. Implied volatility is denoted by the Greek symbol σ, implied volatility increases in bear markets, and it actually decreases when investors are bullish. Implied volatility is a tool that can provide insight into the options future value.

For options traders, more volatility is a good thing. A stock that doesn't have much volatility is going to be a stable stock whose price isn't going to change very much over the lifetime of a contract. So while you may want to sell a covered call for a stock with low volatility, you're probably not going to want to buy one if you're buying call options because that means there will be a lower probability that the stock will change enough to exceed the strike price so you can earn a profit on a trade. Remember too that stocks that are very volatile will attract a lot of interest from options traders and command higher premiums. You will have to do some balancing in picking stocks that are of interest.

Being able to pick stocks that will have the right amount of volatility so that you can be sure of getting one that will earn profits on short term trades is something you're only going to get from experience. You should spend some time practicing before actually investing large amounts of money. That is, pick stocks you are interested in and make your bets but don't actually make the trades. Then follow them over the time period of the contract and see what happens. In the meantime, you can purchase safer call options, and so using this two-pronged approach gain experience that will lead to more surefire success down the road.

One thing that volatility means for everyone is that predicting the future is an impossible exercise. You're going to have some misses no matter how much knowledge and experience you gain. The only thing to aim for is to beat the market more often than you lose. The biggest mistake you can make is putting your life savings into a single stock that you think is a sure thing and then losing it all.

Options to pursue if your options aren't working

At this point, you may think that if the underlying stock for your option doesn't go anywhere or it tanks that you have no choice but to wait out the expiration date and count the money you spend on your premiums as a loss. That really isn't the case. The truth is you can sell a call option you've purchased to other traders in the event it's not working for you. Of course, you're not going to make a profit taking this approach in the vast majority of cases. But it will give you a chance to recoup some of your losses. If you have invested in a large number of call options for a specific stock and it's causing you problems, you need to recoup at least some of your losses may be more acute. Of course, the right course of action in these cases is rarely certain, especially if the expiration date for the contract is relatively far off in the future, which could mean that the stock has many chances to turn around and beat your strike price. Remember, in all bad scenarios actually buying the shares of stock is an option – you're not required to do it. In all cases, the biggest loss you're facing is losing the entire premium. You'll also want to keep the following rule of thumb in mind at all times – the more time value an option has, the higher the price you can sell the option for. If there isn't much time value left, then you're probably going to have to sell the option at a discount. If there is a lot of time value, you may be able to recoup most of your losses on the premium.

Chapter 4. Calls and Puts Options

Put and call options are referred to as a derivative investment. The movements of their prices depend on the movements of prices of a different financial product, also referred to as the underlying.

So, what is an option? It is defined as the right to sell or buy a certain stock with a set price given a specific time frame. With options, you won't have outright ownership of the shares, but you make calculated bets on a stock's price and what its value will be in the future, given the specified expiration of the option. What makes options attractive is that you are to choose whether you want to exercise them or not. If your bet is wrong, you can let the options expire. Although the options' original cost is lost, it still wouldn't compare had you paid for the stock's full price.

Call options are purchased when the trader is expecting the underlying's price to go up within a particular time frame.

Put options are purchased when the trader is expecting the underlying's price to go down within a particular time frame.

There's an option for puts and calls to be written or sold. This will still generate income, but certain rights have to be given up to the option's buyer.

For options defined for the US, a call is defined as an options contract giving the buyer rights to buy an underlying asset at a previously set price any time until the expiration date. For options defined for the EU, buyers can choose to exercise the option to purchase the underlying but only on the set expiration date.

The strike price is defined as a price previously determined at which the call buyer has the choice to purchase the underlying asset. For example, a buyer of a certain stock call option with a 10$ strike price may opt to purchase that stock at the same price before the expiration date of the option.

The expiration of options may vary. It can also be short or long term. It can be worth the while for call buyers to exercise the option, which is to require the writer or seller of the call to sell the stocks at the set strike price., but only if the underlying's current price is more than the strike price. For example, if a stock trades at $10 at the stock market, it is not profitable for the buyer of the call option to exercise the choice to purchase that stock at $11 since they could get the same on the market at a lower price.

Put buyers reserve the right to sell stocks at strike price during a set time range.

The highs and lows the stock market goes through can be both exciting and nerve-wracking for newbie or veteran investors. Risking hard-earned money can make anyone anxious. But played right with sound and well-planned strategies, you can be successful in this field

If you are looking for a way to invest in the stock market but you are trying to avoid the risk of directly selling stocks or buying them, options trading might be perfect for you. Options are typically traded at significantly lower prices compared to the underlying prices of the actual shares. This makes trading them a less risky way to control a large stock position, although you don't own the shares. Using options strategically allows risk mitigation while maintaining huge profit potentials, and you will be playing in the field even if you're investing just a fraction of the stock's price.

All of these benefits of options trading got you excited, right? After all, options have a lower risk and they're a lot cheaper. There are two major disadvantages, however – the limited-time aspect and the reality that you don't own the stock until you choose to exercise your options.

Call Options

With call options, what you pay for is just 'rights to buy' certain shares at a set price and covered by a specific time frame. Let's say that stock ABC is selling for $90 per share in May. If you believe that the stock's price will go up over a few months, you'd purchase a three-month option to buy 100 shares of ABC by August 31 for $100. For this sample call option, you would be paying around $200 if the option cost per share is $2. In options, you are only allowed to buy in increments of 100 shares. This gives you the choice to purchase 100 shares of ABC anytime within the three-month timeframe. The $200 investment is significantly lower than the $9,000 you would have had to shell out if you bought 1000 shares outright.

If you bet right and on July 15, if the ABC shares hit the market at $115, you may exercise the call option and you would have gained $1,300 (that's 100 shares multiplied by the $15 profit you gained per share and deducted by your original investment of $200). If you don't have the resources to buy the shares, you can also make a profit if you re-sell the option to another investor or via the open market. The gain will be pretty much similar to this option.

If you bet wrong, and the price of ABC's shares fell to $80 never to reach $100 within the three-month timeframe, you can let the option reach its expiration, which saves you money (if you bought the shares outright, your original investment of $9,000 is now down to a value of only $8,000, so you lost $1000). This means you only lost $200, which was your investment for the call option.

Risks Involved in Call Options

Like any other form of investment, options have their share of potential risks. Taking the second scenario where you bet wrong as an example and stock ABC never got to $100 during the option's timeframe of three months, you would have lost the entire $200 of your investment, right? In terms of loss percentage, that's %100. Anyone who's been playing the stock market would tell you that it's extremely rare for an investor to suffer a 100% loss. This scenario can only happen if ABC suddenly went bankrupt, causing the price of their stocks to plummet down to zero value.

Therefore, if you look at it from a point of view of percentages, options can cause you huge losses. Let's elaborate on this point. If the price of ABC's share went up to $99 and it's the last day for you to exercise the option, choosing to purchase the shares will mean losing a dollar for each share. What if you invested $9,000 for the stock and you owned 100 stock shares? In three months, which is the option's expiration date if you took it, you would have gained 10% from your original investment ($99 from $90). Comparing both, you would have gained 10% if you purchased the shares outright and lost %100 if you chose the option but did not exercise it. This example shows how risky options can be.

However, the opposite can happen if stock ABC reached a price higher than $100. If you purchased the option, your gain percentage would have been substantially higher compared to buying the stocks outright. If the stock reached $110, you would have gained 400% ($10 gain versus the $2 per share investment) if you went for the option and only gained 22% ($20 gain versus the $90 per share investment) if you purchased the shares.

Lastly, when you own the stock, nothing can force you to sell. That means if after three months, and stock ABC's price goes down, you can hang on to it if you believe it still has the potential to recover and even increase in value compared to the original. If the price goes up dramatically, you'll make significant gains and you didn't incur losses. However, if you chose options as your investment method, the expiration would have forced you to suffer a 100% loss after the set timeframe. There will be no option to hold on to the stock even if you believe it will go up in value soon.

Options have major pros and also major cons. You need to be aware of these before you step into the arena of options trading.

Put Options

On the other side of the options investment is the put option. Whereas call is the right to purchase, 'put' gives you the option to sell a certain security at a set price within a specific time frame. Investors usually purchase put options to protect the price of a stock in case it suddenly drops down, or even the market itself. With put options, you can sell the shares and your investment portfolio is protected from unexpected market swings. Put options are, therefore, a way to hedge your portfolio or lower its risk.

For example, you have invested in stock ABC for 100 shares, which you bought for $50 per share. As of May 31, the price per share has reached a market high $70. Of course, you'd want to maintain this position in your stock, and at the same time protect your gained profits in case the price of this stock goes down. To fit your requirements, you may purchase a put option with a three-month expiration and $70 per share strike price.

If ABC's stock price goes down drastically over the next couple of months, reaching a low per-share price of only $60, you will still be protected. By exercising your put option, you will still be able to sell the shares at $70 each even if stock ABC is now trading at a lower value. If you are feeling confident that ABC can still recover in the future, you can hold on to the stock and just resell the put option. The price of this put option will have gone up because of the diving stock ABC took.

On the other hand, if stock ABC's value kept climbing, just let the put option expire and you would still profit from the increased price of the shares. Even though you lost what you have invested in the put option, you still have the underlying stock with you. Therefore, you can view the put option as a kind of insurance policy for your investment, which may or may not use. Another thing to remember is that you can purchase put options even if you don't own the underlying stock, just like you would in a call option. You are not required to own the stock itself.

Risks Involved in Put Options

Just as with call options, put options carry the same risks. There is also a 100% loss potential when the underlying stock price goes up, and a huge gain when the price dives because you can resell the option for a higher price.

Chapter 5.　The Collar

The collar strategy is an extremely flexible way of trading that you can use for either short term or long-term positions. Mind you, when using it for long term positions, make sure you have substantial unrealized gains already present. This is because the collar imposes a maximum gain limit.

On the flip side, it also caps your downside loss, so this lends itself very well to short term speculative strategies. Mind you, when I say short term, I'm still talking about holding onto the position for at least a month to take advantage of the time decay. From a longer term investment perspective, if you have a position which has made you a lot of money but you're either unsure of how it's going to perform over the short term or are not sure if it will move much further over the long term, you can use the collar to squeeze out the last drops of income from the trade or let it take you out.

This strategy introduces an additional layer on complexity since it has three legs to it:

A long stock positions

A long protective or married put

A short-covered call

In essence, we're adding a long protective put to the covered call strategy. This helps cover the downside and adds to the advantages that a covered call has.

Execution

The first leg to establish is the long stock leg. Like with the covered call, this is an income generator and is entered with the thought of having it increase in value. The second leg to enter is the married put. A married put is a put that covers your downside. Think of it as a stop loss order. Your maximum loss is capped to this level.

The put is bought at an out of the money price (that is below current market levels) at a price that is equal to your maximum risk limit for that position. So, if you think you want to risk a move of just 5 points, then the put is purchased at that price.

Lastly, you need to write an out of the money call just like with the covered call. This call is covered by your long stock position. Make sure you execute your position in this exact order so that you minimize your risk. Let's work through the scenarios on this trade.

If your stock decreases in value, the put below it caps your maximum loss. Once the stock goes below the put's strike price, thereby moving it into the money, that leg is going to be in a profit no matter how low the stock's price goes. If you wish to exit, you sell your stock and you can sell your put which would have increased in value.

Alternatively, if the stock increases in value but doesn't hit your call's strike price before expiry, you earn the premium and the capital gain but are out the amount you paid to buy the put. If the stock does hit the call's strike price, this is your maximum gain possible on the stock leg and you'll have to sell your stock at the call's strike price.

In this case you again earn the capital gains on the long stock leg and the premium on the covered call leg but are out the premium you paid for buying the put. In addition to this, there are alternative scenarios you can encounter.

Let's say the stock declines in value but you're not sure that this is a long-term thing. You feel it's a temporary blip and it'll soon turn upwards. So, what do you do? Should you exit all three positions? Well, this is where the decision to adjust your trade comes into play. You can either reestablish the collar at different prices, which is change the strike prices of the call and the put, or you can exit altogether.

Technical and fundamental analysis should play a part in your decision. For now, just keep in mind that the collar is a wonderfully flexible strategy and with adjustment you can make money even when the trade goes against you or if something unexpected happens.

Now, let's look at an example with real numbers to see how it all plays out.

Example

Sticking with GOOG, we see that the market price is still $1229. So as a first step, in case this is a speculative position, we establish the long stock leg. Next, we establish the long put or protective put. Which price should you choose? Remember, this is an option purchase, so you'll need to pay to enter the position.

The temptation will be to enter at as low a price as possible since you're going to lose this money no matter what happens (if it moves into the money or remains out of the money you lose the option premium no matter what). Resist the temptation to look at this in monetary terms.

Instead look at it in terms of risk involved. Your put's strike price will dictate your maximum position size. You need to decide what your necessary risk per trade amount is going to be. This can be a function of either a percentage of your overall capital or a fixed amount.

Once this is done, you divide this amount by the points between your put and the long stock entry point and this gives you your position size. Simple math really. Place your put at a level beyond the closest support which you think is going to hold. The idea is to not have this put move into the money, not minimize the cost you pay.

Remember that this trade is only going to last a little beyond a month so don't go searching for the stronger support out there. Simply pick the most appropriate one given the current balance in the market. For example, if it's in a range, simply pick a level which is beyond the lower range boundary.

Let's say you decide to enter GOOG at the current market price and that an appropriate put level is 1200. Looking at GOOG's option chain, we see that the October 25th, 1200 put is selling for $25.20. So, this amount is going to go out of pocket, in addition to whatever you paid for the long stock.

Now, we search for an appropriate level to write our call. It is yielding the same price as before and that is $16. We will receive this amount no matter what.

Hence, our cost of entry equals:

Cost of entry = cost of long stock price + cost of put premium - premium received from short call = 1229+25.2-16 = 1238.20 per share

You'll notice how the cost on entry actually increases with this method as opposed to a straight long stock purchase. Well, this is the price you pay for the additional protection. If you were to merely protect your downside via a put, your breakeven price would increase by the value of the put premium. In this case, that works out to $25.20.

So, the covered call reduces your breakeven price quite significantly while maintaining your downside as intended. All in all, you pay a few dollars more for this privilege which is a good deal overall. Now that we know our cost of entry, what is our maximum loss?

Maximum loss = Long stock entry - Put strike price - premium from call + put premium paid = 1229-1200-16+25.2 = $38.20 per share.

If you placed a stop loss order at the put's strike price wouldn't that cover your downside for a lesser amount? Yes, but remember that the put insulates you from the possibility of the market price jumping your stop loss level thanks to a lack of liquidity or excess volatility. So, there is a price to pay for this protection. Let's see how your maximum gain is affected.

Maximum gain = Call strike price - Long stock entry price - put entry premium + call writing premium = 1270-1229-25.2+16 = $31.80 per share

In these calculations, the premiums you pay and receive for the options skew the numbers quite a lot. In reality, a lot of options strategies do not take the premiums paid into account when figuring out the maximum gain and risk because this is a cash expense. However, I'm illustrating these here just to show you how it affects the numbers.

So, it looks like you're risking a larger amount than what you stand to gain when you take the premiums into account. Two things about this: this is just an example and I've assumed certain price levels, so this is not fully reflective of the strategy. Second, this highlights the importance of picking a good put and call strike price level since the premiums do skew the numbers quite a lot.

This is why it's extremely important for you to brush up on your technical analysis skills prior to trading collars. You can get away with imperfect knowledge when it comes to the covered call since that has a large long stock leg which makes you all the money. However, over here your holding time is shorter, and your transaction costs are higher.

Hence, get to know the stock you're trading deeply and simulate collars on it before going live. The collar should really be the cornerstone of your options trading strategy so make sure you master this before moving onto the other strategies in this book. In terms of progression, I would say do not move ahead until you're making steady money with collars.

On the plus side, once you've established the collar, it needs no maintenance and pretty much takes care of itself. This doesn't mean you switch off from the market completely. I'd suggest checking in at least once a day, which is the minimum required for passive trading strategies.

The collar as you can see is a long-biased strategy. Is it possible to have a bearish collar? Well, yes, it is actually. Now that you've grasped the basics of the execution required as well as the math that underlies the strategy, let's look at what to do in case you wish to adjust the trade.

Adjustments

So, you've entered a collar and promptly the price dives below your entry and brings your put into the money. What now? You were envisioning holding onto the position for at least a month but here you are, less than a day in the trade, and you're already facing the prospect of hitting your maximum loss.

The first thing to do is to evaluate whether your technical assumptions are still valid. If your technical analysis was spot on, usually there will be some fundamental event you have overlooked. Is your stock dependent on the bond market, unbeknownst to you? Check your assumptions once again and see if your entry logic still holds water. If it doesn't, eat the loss and move on. Chalk it up to the cost of tuition of learning how to trade.

By the way, expect to do this sort of thing quite a lot when you're starting out. Trading is not an easy endeavor, and this is why you should make as many of your mistakes in simulation, while demoing your strategies, instead of jumping into a live account and sabotaging yourself.

Assuming your initial conclusions are still valid, perhaps this is a temporary downswing in an effort to shakeout the weaker long traders. In such cases, you can seek to reestablish your collar. First, sell your put position and determine what will be a more appropriate level to reenter. When you sell your put, you'll make money on that leg since it would have moved into the money.

Chapter 6. Vertical Spread

When it comes to spread trading, there are two categories all types of trades fit into. These are vertical spreads and horizontal spreads. The names sound fancy but understanding how they work really isn't anywhere near as complicated.

Having said that, these types of trades do crank the complexity level up a bit. If the collar took things up a notch from covered calls then spread trades do the same with the collar. As beneficial as collars and covered calls are there is one major disadvantage that those strategies pose to the trader.

They require a long stock purchase. In the case of a covered call this is an investment while in the case of a collar it can be speculative or an investment. Whatever the designation there's no escaping the fact that long stock investment requires a lot of money. What if you wish to emulate Thales' example and get in on low capital values?

This is what the spread strategies address. Options give us the flexibility to play around with the way price moves and as you'll see, spread trades encompass taking advantage of a wide variety of market behavior.

Bull Call Spreads

The first type of vertical spread we'll be looking at is the bull call spread. This is a bullish trading strategy and works best in the middle portions of trending markets. I'll address why this is so. For now, keep in mind that while this is a bullish strategy it works best when bullishness is beginning to slow down, and you observe the ranges getting larger.

You can utilize this in the earlier, more forceful, part of trends but this isn't the most efficient use of it. In those portions, you're better off simply buying a call and letting its premium rise. The covered call works well in those environments too.

Either way, the bull call spread has two legs to it. You will be buying one call and selling another. Thus, the long call leg of the trade covers the short call. Let's take a look at the legs in more details

Trade Legs

The first leg you should establish is the long call leg. This needs to be an at the money or sightly out of the money call that you're sure will move into the money soon. The objective is to use this leg to make the majority of the profit in this trade. In essence, you're substituting the long stock position from the previous two strategies with a long call position.

Establishing a long stock position meant that you needed to protect it somehow which is why we had to incorporate a third leg in the case of the collar. With the covered call, given the investment nature of the trade, downside protection is moot since you'll be holding onto it for the long term anyway and the objective is to hold onto your investment no matter how much it dips (assuming the dip isn't catastrophic.)

The second leg of the bull call spread is the short call. This is written out of the money at a point where you think price will advance to, even if it does so sluggishly. Much like with every other strategy we've looked at, you want both of these options to expire at least 30 days or more from the trade date. This helps you capture and avoid the risk of time decay.

Like the collar, the bull call spread can be adjusted, and its greatest power lies in a good adjustment. This allows you to remain in the market at low cost. Adjustments depend on what the market scenario looks like. You should deploy this in times when bullishness is starting to be challenged by bearishness and thus, you will enter with the knowledge that the trend is still strong but there are some headwinds ahead.

You should place your short call at a level beyond the most relevant resistance ahead. Once price breaches this level, you should move it a few points higher to where the next resistance level could potentially be and so on. Alternatively, if you feel that the counter trend presence is becoming far too much, you could let the market take you out of the position and close your long and cover your short position.

Bull Put Spread

The bull put spread strategy seeks to take advantage of the exact same set of market conditions that the bull call spread seeks. So, what is the difference between the two? Aside from the obvious fact that one strategy uses calls and the other uses puts, there are many subtleties that you ought to be aware of.

The strategies do not contradict one another, in case you're wondering. Think of it as having two choices to pursue depending on what market conditions look like. If you're wondering how to determine the conditions which are ideal for each strategy, then the first step is to take a look at the bull put spread and understand how it works.

Trade Legs

Like the bull call, the bull put is a two-legged trade. The first leg involves establishing a long-put position which is out of the money and is below a strong support level. This long put is what caps your downside risk in case things go wrong. In addition to this, the long put also covers the next leg.

This is a short put which is written near or at the money. This leg is the primary profit driving instrument for the trade. I'd like to

58

point out here that the structure and positioning of the puts is very different from that of the calls. With the bull call spread, you were capping your maximum gain on the trade by writing an OTM call.

Here's you're not capping any gains and are in fact capping your loss via a trade leg. In the bull call spread, your maximum loss was automatically capped as a part of the trade structure. You could argue that this is what is happening here as well but it's pretty clear that the way in which the strategies do this is very different.

The next major point of difference is in the results trade entry gives you. The bull call is net debit trade, but the bull put is a net credit trade. Net debit trades have you realize your maximum loss upon trade entry. Net credit trades realize your maximum gain upon entry. This means, you earn your maximum profit on entry and if all goes well, your options will maintain themselves.

Like the bull call spread, you can adjust the trade depending on market conditions. Given that your upside is not capped, adjustments will need to be made primarily if the market turns downwards and if you see your puts move into the money. In this case, you will need to readjust the spread lower and exit your primary position. Thus, the adjustment scenarios in the bull put strategy aren't as varied as they are in the others we've seen so far.

If the trade works in your favor, you can establish a higher spread using the same principles you used to establish the initial one.

Bear Call Spread

If you can use call spreads to take advantage of bullish conditions, you can use them to take advantage of bearish ones as well. In case you're wondering, it is possible to do this with puts as well and much like what we saw with the bullish spreads, you have a choice of using either call or put spreads to do this. For now, let's take a look at bear call spreads.

The bear call spread has two legs to it, much like the bull spreads do. As the name suggests you'll be setting up calls as part of this strategy. Let's take a deeper look at the two legs now.

Trade Legs

The first leg you want to establish is a long call position. The long call is placed at a level that is beyond a resistance zone and is the leg that limits your risk. The call itself is placed out of the money. The further away the call is, the greater your risk in the trade is.

The second leg to establish is the primary profit driving leg of this trade. This is a short call you will write as close to the money as possible. The exact placement of this level is a tricky thing since you don't want it to move into the money. If it does, you'll have to wind up both legs of the trade and take your maximum loss amount.

Bear call spreads are net credit trades which means you'll capture your entire gain upon trade entry. As such, like other options trading strategies we've seen thus far, you don't need to do anything special to maintain the trade. You can adjust it as well but given that this is a net credit trade, there isn't much you can do in terms of adjustment beyond working out another spread level in case the original trade doesn't work out.

Bear Put Spread

The bear put spread is the bearish cousin of the bull call spread in that it is a net debit trade that seeks to capture more of the upside in a bearish movement. By now, hopefully you've got a hang of how vertical spread trades are setup so let's quickly run through how this trade works.

Like the other three it has two legs to it: A long put and a short put. The long put is established at the money or as near to the money as possible and is the primary profit driver in this trade. The short put is written out of the money, a few levels below and functions as a profit target of sorts.

The aim with this trade, like with the bull call spread is to capture as much of the market movement as possible. Hence, adjustments play an important role here. Once the market moves close to your short call, you can adjust your target downwards and move your long call leg up.

The timeline for this trade is the same as that of the others. You're looking at establishing options that are at least 30 days or so away from the trade entry date in order to avoid or capture as much of

61

the time decay as possible. Using our TSLA example with a market price of $478.15, let's assume that we write the TSLA 450 option expiring a month from now.

This will net us $23.90 in premiums. We can go long on the 475 put which will cost us $36.05. Thus, the net debit on the trade and our maximum loss is $12.15. Our maximum gain is limited to the strike price of the OTM put and this is $25.

Chapter 7. Horizontal Spread

Here are some horizontal spreads that traders should know about.

Calendar Call Spread Strategy

The spreads we've seen thus far have been what are called vertical spreads. This implies how they show up on the option chain, where strike prices are listed on top of one another. By shorting one and buying another, you're earning the difference in the prices of the two and hence the term' spread'.

Vertical spreads require you to trade options within the same expiration month but horizontal spreads, which is what the calendar spread is, involves buying and selling options form different expiration months. The call calendar spread is a bullish strategy that can be used to great effect as we'll see.

Execution

The calendar call spread consists of two legs:

A current month or short-term short call

A near month or longer-term long call

The idea is that while the stock takes its time to make it to the longer (time frame) call's strike price, you might as well collect the premium on the short call in the meantime. The instrument for profit is the longer call which captures the upward movement in the stock.

The longer-term call can be from the near month or something from the longer cycle. The choice is yours. The only consideration here is the liquidity since you don't want to be trading in an instrument which has a huge spread thanks to low demand or trading volume. As long as the liquidity is fine and spreads are low or manageable, you should be fine.

As your first step to implementing the trade, you will purchase an at or in the money call in anticipation of the move upwards. The short call is at a level you think the price is not going to reach within that time frame. The idea is to earn the premium from the short call and the capital gain from the long call. If this trade works out, it is as close to a win-win as you can get in the markets. Let's see how the math works with AMZN.

Let's say our long call is from the near month. The price we'll pay for the 1830 call, which is the one nearest to market price and in the money is $63.65. For our short call, let's say there a medium level resistance at 1840, which AMZN is going to have to work to get past and is unlikely to do this by the end of the month.

The premium we earn on this call is $36.30.

The cost of entry = Cost of long call - premium earned from short call = 63.65-36.3 = $27.35 per share.

Maximum loss = cost of entry

There are many scenarios for calculating the maximum gain as you can imagine since this depends on whether the short-term call ever moves into the money. Whatever the scenario, you will have to subtract your cost of entry from the final gain.

Horizontal spreads are thus different from vertical spreads thanks to their open-ended nature. It will take some getting used to, but with time, you'll find that they tend to be far more rewarding if you can get your analysis correct.

Put Calendar Spread

The horizontal put spread is similar in premise to the call calendar spread except it seeks to take advantage of a bearish market. The structure of the trade is also similar to call. It's just that you'll be buying puts instead of calls. There are two legs that are a part of the trade.

The short put leg is placed at a strike price that is beyond a support level that is medium in strength. It will have an expiry date that is beyond 30 days out but less than the expiry date of the second, long put leg. The long put will have the same strike price as the short put.

The idea is to capture the benefits of the short-term neutral behavior and the long-term bearishness. The shorter term, short put provides a premium and the long term put provides capital gains in the form of increases in intrinsic value as prices dive. This is also a net debit trade.

Much like the call calendar spread, the put spread can be adjusted as well depending on the type of market behavior observed. The most common adjustment methods involve converting it into a vertical spread to take advantage of price behavior.

This concludes our look at horizontal spread trades. As you can see, they're not very complex in nature and are far easier to maintain and understand than vertical spread trades. Spread trades are a step up from collars and like the collar, they offer decent and steady rewards when executed correctly.

Chapter 8. Strangles and Straddles

Doing this requires some attention on your part. You are going to have to think ahead in order to implement this strategy and profit from it. Remember that you can use a straddle or strangle any time that you think the stock is going to make a major shift one way or the other. An example of a non-earning season situation, where this could be a useful strategy, would be a new product announcement. Think Apple. If Apple is having one of their big presentations, if the new phone that comes out disappoints the analysts, share prices are probably going to drop by a large amount. On the other hand, if it ends up surprising viewers with a lot of new features that make it the must-have phone again, this will send Apple stock soaring.

The problem here is you really don't know which way it's going to go. There are going to be leaks and rumors but basing your trading decisions on that is probably not a good approach, often, the rumors are wrong. A strangle or straddle allows you to avoid that kind of situation and make money either way.

Other situations that could make this useful include changes in management or any political interaction. We mentioned the government recently made a privacy settlement with Facebook. If you knew when the settlement was going to occur but wasn't sure what it was going to be, using a strangle or straddle might be a good way to earn money from the large price moves that were sure to follow.

The same events that might warrant buying a long call such as a GDP number or jobs report, for options on index funds, are also appropriate for strangles and straddles.

Implied Volatility Strategy

Implied volatility is very important when a big event like an earnings report is coming. This gives you a way to make profits. In fact, we are going to call this the implied volatility strategy.

Let's review how this would work. Remember, implied volatility is a projection of what the volatility of the stock is going to be in the near future. When there is an earnings call, the volatility is going to be extreme on the day after the call. Therefore, you are going to see the implied volatility growing as earnings day approaches.

At the time I am writing this, it is 24 hours before Facebook's earnings call. The implied volatility is 74%, which is very high. In contrast, for Apple, which is more than a week away from its next earnings call, the implied volatility is only 34%. This is for a $207.50 strike put, with a share price of $207.9.

The strategy is to profit from the implied volatility. You want to enter your position one to two weeks before the earnings call or big announcement. As implied volatility increases, this is going to swamp out time decay and cause a big rise in the option price.

Using that Apple put option, if we assumed that there were only 4 days to expiration, but the implied volatility had risen to about where Facebook is and there were no other changes (so we will leave the share price where it was), the price of the put option would increase by about $330.

So, if nothing else, you could profit from the change of implied volatility. It will probably go highest the day before the earnings call.

This is going to be magnified if you trade a strangle or straddle. Prior to the earnings call, both the put and the call option are going to increase a great deal in value because of implied volatility. So, you could sell the strangle the day before the earnings call and book some profits then. Since a strangle or straddle can earn big profits if there is a large move in the share price, you won't find any problems locating a buyer.

Estimating Price from Implied Volatility

If you know the implied volatility, you can make an estimate of the price range of the stock. This can be done using a simple formula.

(Stock price x implied volatility)/SQRT (days in a year)

If you don't want to do the calculation, if we take the square root of 365, it is about 19.1. For example, we use Facebook with a share price of $202.50 and an implied volatility of 76%.

Facebook	
Stock Price	$202.50
Implied Vol.	0.76
Days in a year	19.1049732
Expected Change	$8.06
Upper Range	$210.56
Lower Range	$194.44

The implied volatility gives us an idea of what traders are thinking, in regard to the upcoming earnings call, but of course, we can never be sure what is really going to happen until it does. But this gives us upper and lower bounds. Using the information that we have available, we can guess that Facebook might rise to $210.56 a share after the earnings call, or it might drop to $194.44 per share after the earnings call. You can use these boundaries to set up your strategy. However, remember that if there is a big surprise, it can go well past these boundary points in one direction or the other.

What is a Long Straddle?

To set up a straddle, you buy a put option and a call option simultaneously (buy = take a long position). The maximum loss that you can incur is the sum of the cost to buy the call option plus the sum of the cost to buy the put option. This loss is incurred when you enter the trade.

With a straddle, you buy a call option and a put option together. And they would be with the same strike price. By necessity, this means that one option is going to be in the money and one option is going to be out of the money. When approaching an earnings call, the prices can be kind of steep, because you want to price them close to the current share price. That way, it gives us some room to profit either way the stock price moves.

A maximum loss is only incurred if you hold the position to expiration. You can always choose to sell it early, if it looks like it's not going to work out and take a loss that is less than the maximum.

There is a total premium paid for entering into the position. This is the amount of cash paid for buying the call added to the money paid for buying the put. This is called the total premium. There are two breakeven points:

To the upside, the breakeven point is the strike price + total premium paid.

On the downside, the breakeven point is the strike price − total premium paid.

It the price of the stock moves up past the breakeven point, the put is worthless. However, the call option would earn substantial profits. On the other hand, if the stock price moved down past the lower price point, that would be the breakeven, the call option would be worthless and the put option would earn substantial profits.

For example, suppose that we buy a $207.5 straddle on Apple 7 days to expiration with an implied volatility of 35%, and the underlying price is $207. The total cost to enter the position is $8.03 ($803 total). At 1 day to expiration, the share price breaks up to $220 a share after the earnings call. The put expires worthless, but the call jumps to $12.50. The net profit is then $12.50 - $8.03 = $4.47, or $447 in total per contract.

If instead, the share price had dropped to $190, the call expires worthless, and the put jumps to $17.50 per share. The net profit, in this case, is then $17.50 - $8.03 = $9.47 per share or a total of $947.

This isn't to say that the straddle would be more profitable for a stock decrease, it is not. The profit will be the same no matter which way the share price moves, in our examples, we used two different sized moves. The point is to illustrate that no matter which direction the stock moves, you can profit.

If the stock is at the money at expiration, we could still recoup some of the investment and sell the straddle for a loss. In this case, the call and the put would both be priced at $152. We'd still be at a loss, but we could recoup $304 by selling both at $152.

Short Straddle

If you sell a straddle, then you are taking the opposite position, which means you would be betting that the share price stays inside the range and hope that the stock didn't make a big move to the upside or the downside. To sell a straddle you'd have to either be able to do a covered call and protected put or be a level 4 trader who could sell naked options.

Long Strangle

A strangle is similar to a straddle, but in this case, the strike prices are different. In this case, you will buy a just barely out of the money call option, while simultaneously buying a slightly out of the money put option. The two options will have the same expiration date. The breakeven points for a strangle are going to be calculated in a similar way as the breakeven prices for a straddle, but you are going to use the individual strike prices for the call and put because they are different. So, you calculate the total premium paid, which is the total amount paid for the call option plus the premium paid for the put option. Then the breakeven points are given by the following formulas:

To the upside, the breakeven point is the strike price of the call + total premium paid.

On the downside, the breakeven point is the strike price of the put – total premium paid.

In a similar fashion as compared to a long straddle, the maximum loss is going to occur when the share price ends up in between the two strike prices. Therefore, you might want to choose strike prices that are relatively close, in order to minimize the range over which the loss can occur. Of course, there is a tradeoff here because the closer in range the strike prices are, the more expensive it is going to be in order to enter the position. But, it's going to increase your probability of profit because if the strike prices are tight about the current share price, there is a higher probability that the share prices are going to exceed the call strike + premium paid, or decrease below the put strike price less the price paid to enter the contract (the premium).

Chapter 9. Greeks

When you begin options trading, you are going to encounter some mysterious parameters called "the Greeks." These are five pieces of data that accompany every option, and they are denoted with Greek letters. The designations used are a result of the mathematical formulas that go into options pricing, but don't let that put you off. In reality, the Greeks are pretty straightforward, and you don't have to follow all of the Greeks in your analysis of what options to trade. Many options traders don't pay much attention to the Greeks, but as a more informed options investor, you are going to want to, at least, be aware of them and check their values.

Greeks Change in Real-Time

The first thing to know about the Greeks before we get started looking at them in detail is that they change in real-time. So, if someone tells you that delta is 0.5 or 0.62, it doesn't mean these are going to be the values that you see by the time you look at the option. As the stock trades all day long, and the value of the share price changes, the values of the Greeks are going to change as well. The magnitude of those changes may or may not be small, depending on what is going on with the markets. This is just something to keep in mind and to be aware of as we discuss each of the Greeks.

As we go about discussing the Greeks, I am going to be listing them in the order of importance as I see it. Not all options traders will agree, so you can take my listings with a bit of a grain of salt. But nonetheless, this will help you to understand what they are, their meaning, and how important they are to your trading.

Delta

The first Greek that we are going to encounter is named for the Greek letter delta. This parameter tells you how the price of an option is going to change with respect to a change in the share price of the underlying stock. It is listed as a decimal number that ranges from 0.0 – 1.0.

The dividing line for delta is 0.50, which is the value delta would have for an option that was exactly at the money. So, what does this mean? It means that if the price, for instance, goes up by an increment of $1.00, you are looking at a call option that is $0.50 more. So, if the share price of Disney happened to be $132, and you possess a call option having the exact price, if the share price went up to $132.50, the price of the call option would go up by $0.25. On the other hand, if the share price had risen to $133, the value of the call option would have risen by $0.50.

While traders like to focus on gains, this cut both ways. So, if the stock dropped from $132 a share to $131 a share, your option would drop in value by $0.50.

Remember that options prices are quoted on a per-share basis, but they are for 100 shares of stock. That means that a 50-cent drop is quite significant. If you're looking at an option that is priced at $100, a 50 cent drop in share price could translate into a drop in the price of the option of $25. And of course, if it rose by $0.50, you'd make $25 on the option.

Put options have a negative delta. This reflects the fact that the correlation between the put's value and the fluctuation in the share's price is in the opposite manner. That is, if the price of the stock goes up, the put option loses value. If it's another way around; that is, the stock loses its favorable spot in the market, the put options become lucrative when traded. But the meaning is the same.

So, when you are looking at an at the money put option, you are going to see a delta of -0.50. If the price of the stock rises by $1, you will lose fifty cents per share on the option. In contrast, if the stock dropped by $1 in value, you would gain fifty cents.

If an option is deemed to be "in the money," it creates a favorable condition, with the delta having a value of 0.50+. We can say that the delta responds well to the money conditions. Remember that delta's value goes up the more the option reaches the in the money condition. If Disney is trading at $130.50, we find that a $129 call option has a delta of 0.7149. A $122 call has a delta of 0.9449.

Theta

The second Greek that you want to keep an eye on is theta. This is a measure of time decay for the option. Theta is always negative. This reflects the fact that as time goes on, the value of the option that is tied up in time value declines. The time value of an option always declines; the question is only by what amount. You can look up theta to determine the amount. As stocks are traded throughout the day, the value of theta is going to change. However, the way that you are going to feel theta is when the days pass. So, at each market open on a new trading day, options will lose extrinsic value. The amount of value that they lose will be equal to the value of theta.

If you look up an option that is priced at $1 (per share), and you see theta is -0.11, at market open, the value of the option will drop to $0.89. In real terms, if you had bought the option for $100, it would drop in value to $89.

That illustrates how theta works. It's going to make its impact felt at the market open. Options do not lose time value during the day; it's the number of days to expiration that is important. The fewer the number of days left to expiration, the less time value the option has. As it loses value each day, we say that the option is experiencing time decay. All options go through time decay, no matter what. Since it's the number of trading days left to expiration that determines this, it only applies as the market opens.

However, time decay is not the only thing impacting options pricing. Suppose that delta for some call option that was $1 at the previous market close is 0.65, and theta is -0.11. If the share price were to rise a dollar at market open, that means delta and theta would add up to determine the new options price. So, it would go up 65 cents from delta but drops 11 cents from theta. So, you would have a net increase of 54 cents, and the option would now be priced at $1.54.

This exercise illustrates the fact that in order to estimate the future price of an option, you need to know everything that's going on. Even if there was no increase in share price at the market open, you might ignore the 11-cent drop. That's because it is going to be the only drop due to theta throughout the coming trading day, and a lot can happen throughout the day. A small move in stock price can easily make up for the drop in price due to time decay, and by the middle of the day, you might not even notice that you had lost that $11 off the value of the option.

However, you definitely need to account for that loss, so theta is not something to ignore. If the option is out of the money, it's going to be harder to make up for the value lost in the option due to time decay.

Vega

The third most important Greek (in my opinion) is vega. This Greek parameter tells you how sensitive the option is to changes in implied volatility. Precisely, the value of vega estimates how the price of the option is going to change in response to a 1% change in the implied volatility of the underlying stock. Under normal conditions, vega may not be that important. While you can look up the volatility for a given stock by looking at its beta parameter (note that beta is for the stock itself, not for options), that gives you the long-term volatility of the stock. Over short time periods, under most conditions, the volatility is not going to change all that much.

Before the earnings call, nobody knows for certain which way the shares are going to move. People will be engaging in a lot of speculation, but that speculation could be wrong. Furthermore, even if there is an earnings report that is good or bad, nobody can be quite sure how the market is going to react. Sometimes, the market won't react at all. But that doesn't matter prior to the earnings call because it's the implied volatility that we are concerned about when it comes to options.

As such, in the two weeks prior to an earnings call, you will see options prices spike from increases in implied volatility, and this phenomenon will reach a maximum right before the earnings call.

You can profit from this by purchasing options a week or two prior to the calls and selling them when prices have risen enough to make the levels of profits that you are looking for.

So implied volatility is one thing to keep in mind when trading options. It is not always going to be significant, but there are times, like in earnings calls, when you are going to want to pay more attention to it and possibly utilize it in your trading strategy.

Rho

Next, we come to rho, which is a Greek parameter related to the risk-free interest rate. As we touched on in the first part, the risk-free interest rate is usually taken to be the interest rate on a 10-year U.S. Treasury bill. What is important for options is not the interest rate itself but how it is changing. Rising interest rates can make options less attractive because capital tends to leave the stock market and go into bonds when interest rates are rising by large amounts. In today's environment, and, in fact, over the past 20 years, this hasn't been too much of a concern. Interest rates have been at record low levels over the past decade, as government officials have been trying to use low-interest rates to prop up the economy. Whether that actually works or not is not our concern here, but the fact of the matter is they have only tentatively raised interest rates at times that they have considered doing so, which means that the impact on the stock market has been minimal.

Gamma

The final Greek is called gamma. Simply put, or maybe not simply put if you are not mathematically minded, gamma is the rate of change of delta. Technically, it's the second derivative. It tells you how rapidly delta is going to change with changes in stock prices. While hardcore options traders are going to be paying attention to this, most options traders don't need to keep a close eye on gamma. Beginning options traders are probably only going to be looking at delta and theta, and my experience is that delta provides the real information that you need when it comes to the sensitivity of the option to changing stock prices. Rather than following gamma, you are better off keeping tabs on the delta in real-time. The odds are that delta is not going to change much unless there is a very large change in stock prices.

Conclusion

One of the leading ways of gaining financial freedom is setting up passive income streams. Trading options has the potential to be a powerful form of passive income. Not only does this activity give the trader the platform to gain financial freedom but it also allows the trader to pursue hobbies, career options and other activities that he or she loves. It allows this because the trader is not actively trading time for money. Options traders have the flexibility to live and work anywhere in the world because, when done right, trading options allows the trader to earn tens of thousands of dollars and more even while he or she sleeps.

This book was written as a comprehensive guide to show that any and every one can earn a sizable income from options trading as long as this person is willing to develop a growth mindset, learn from the mistakes and successes of other traders and work to put in that human and financial investment upfront. Options are derivative contracts that allow the owner of the contract the right to buy or sell the associated asset by an expiration date specified. From this definition, you can see that this is not something you simply dabble in every now and then.

Stock market investment is one of the best ways to protect your hard-earned money. During recession, most of the companies struggled to keep their heads above water, and the majority of the regular citizens started to protect their savings from irreparable loss. Most of the regular stock buyers started to walk away from the share markets, but few people who are intelligent purchased the shares which were at an unbelievable lower price. When the stock value of big companies fall you can purchase the stock at a lower price, and it is the best time to buy shares.

Lightning Source UK Ltd.
Milton Keynes UK
UKHW022032301222
414666UK00005B/25